rocketship to the
andromeda galaxy

m a r c   v i n c e n z

Spuyten Duyvil
New York City

ISBN 978-1-963908-43-5

Cover design, artwork, book design, typography, concept, words, tonics and sonics by Marc Vincenz.

All images courtesy of NASA and the Space Telescope Science Institute, except for the photo of Löwenmensch by Dagmar Hollmann and the photo of the Kish Tablet by Locutus Borg aka José-Manuel Benito.

Found in the Hohle Fels in the Swabian Jura of Germany, Löwenmensch (Lion-being) has been dated to around 42,000 BCE. Carved from a single piece of mammoth tusk, this sculpture is one of the oldest-known representations of figurative art.

Dated to approximately 3500 BCE, the Kish Tablet is a limestone tablet from the Mesopotamian city of Kish, and is currently considered to be the first known evidence of writing.

The image on the back cover, The Pillars of Creation, *was taken by the James Webb Space Telescope in 2022 and is located in the Serpens constellation—around 7000 light years from where we currently reside.*

101 copies signed by the author

for every last Earthling
orbiting their own spacetime

Some Cooling Perspective

Apparently, in one billion years, before Mother Earth bursts into a quadrillion fragments, we will be a world boiling over at ten thousand degrees.

Some Warming Perspective

And thus, our fated ancestors, the last ten thousand, shall be dozing in stasis for light years waiting to populate another warming planet.

Cerebral Cortex

How quickly autumn burns through your face.

How quickly winter pales.

Neural Integration

How you burst into singsong when the sun
appears behind your head like a halo, and the
shadows at your feet dance like tiny gods.

Almost a Fortunate Footnote

And no less so for trying not to.

Non-living Matter

As mountain streams begin to feed the soil,
they resurface again to the moon-locked eon.

Something Like Time and a God

What better way to get here than in golden
armor on the backs of fire-breathing dragons;
in such a fashion, one is portrayed as pertinent
in the schemata of history.

Better Iconography

There will be statues and paintings and comparisons with tiny gods.

No More Time

There was no such clock.

There was no such time.

Failed Nursery Rhyme

As the butcher's wife dissected the room, the mice pranced ahead and then slipped into the oak skirting behind the burning stove.

Central Nervous System

It was as if the tiny gods had mumbled, then tumbled straight through our essences like radiation through rock and mantle.

A Belief System

And no, our selves we were not connecting
at first, but when we started praying, a new
world was seeded from water and light.

Natural Neurotoxins

The air is warm and good here.

The trees are heavy with love.

A Fresh Start

Creatures swarm through the sky.

Clouds gather in battle formations.

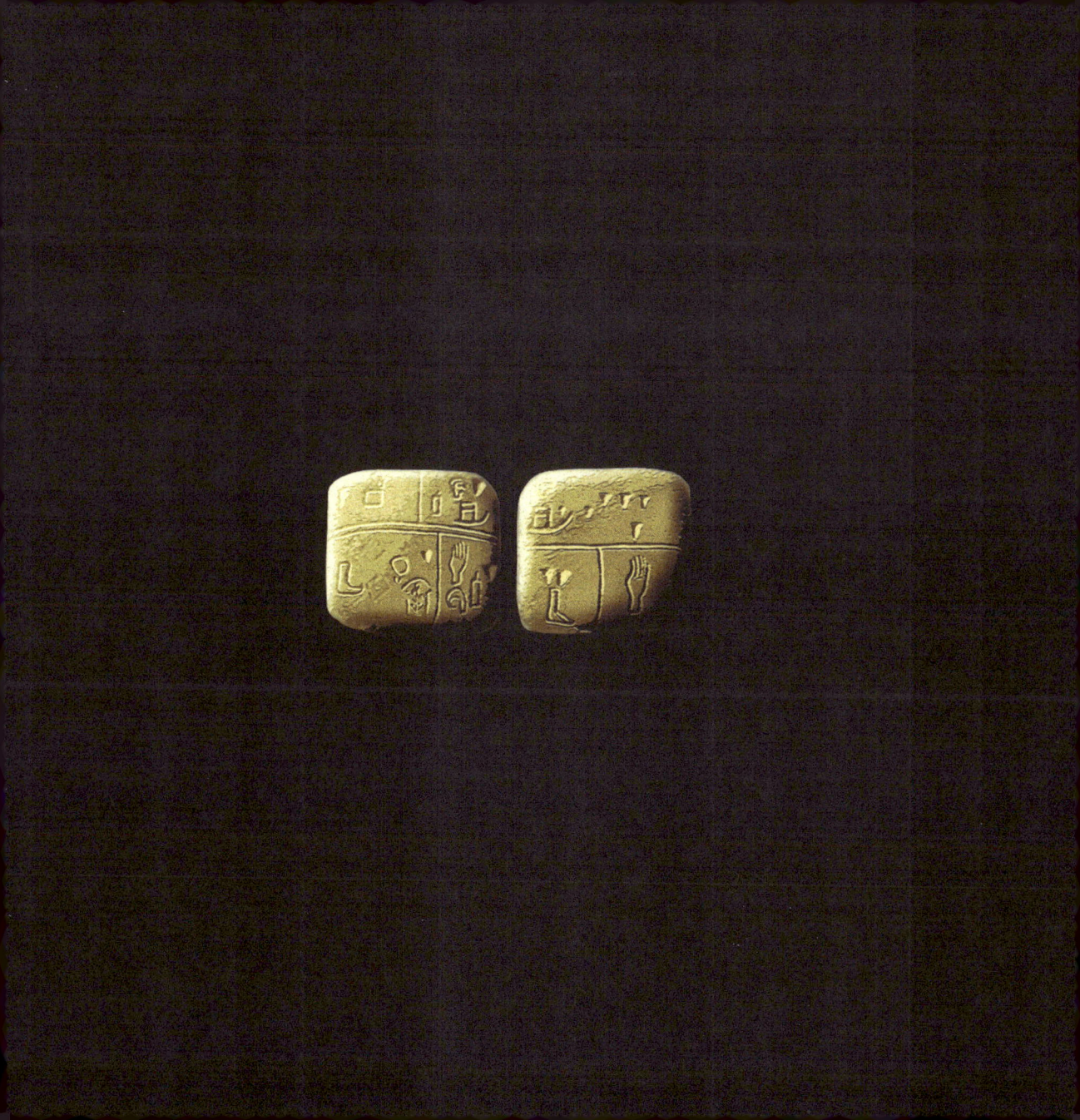

The Author

Marc Vincenz is a poet, fiction writer, translator, editor, musician and artist. He has published many books of poetry, fiction and translation. His more recent poetry collections include *The Pearl Diver of Irunmani*, *A Splash of Cave Paint*, *The King of Prussia is Drunk on Stars* and *Spells for the Wicked*.

His translation of Swiss poet Klaus Merz' selected poems, *An Audible Blue*, won the 2023 Massachusetts Book Award for Translation. He is publisher and editor of MadHat Press and publisher of *New American Writing* and lives on a farm in Western Massachusetts where there are more spiny-nosed voles, tufted grey-buckle hares and *Amoeba scintilla* than Earthlings.

www.ingramcontent.com/pod-product-compliance
Lightning Source LLC
Chambersburg PA
CBHW041623120626
46551CB00003B/561